G000270149

Shrewsbury

IN OLD PHOTOGRAPHS

This view of St Chad's Church was photographed by Arthur Knight, a local businessman, around 1900. Mr Knight's hobby has left us with a number of interesting shots of Shrewsbury, several of which are included in this volume. St Chad's was rebuilt on this site after the fall of the old church on Belmont in 1788. Its unusual circular plan was the creation of George Steuart. Both the site and the design caused a great deal of controversy in the town at the time. The wall that runs along St Chad's Terrace was replaced in 1906 and was a gift of the Horticultural Society.

Shrewsbury

IN OLD PHOTOGRAPHS

DAVID TRUMPER

Alan Sutton Publishing Limited
Phoenix Mill · Far Thrupp · Stroud
Gloucestershire

First Published 1994

Copyright © David Trumper, 1994

To Vicki

British Library Cataloguing in Publication Data.
A catalogue record for this book is available from
the British Library.

ISBN 0–7509–0704–5

Typeset in 9/10 Sabon.
Typesetting and origination by
Alan Sutton Publishing Limited.
Printed in Great Britain by
Ebenezer Baylis, Worcester.

A balloon glides over the town one Flower Show day in the 1920s. On the skyline we see the spires of St Mary's and St Alkmund's and the tower of St Julian's. In the foreground is the clock tower of the old Market Hall. The tower rose to a height of 151 ft and housed a bell which bore the following inscription that was penned by Henry Pidgeon, a local historian: 'My sounding voice time's passing hour proclaims, O'er Salop Town and Severn's fertile plains.'

Contents

Pride Hill & Castle Street, Shrewsbury.

From the

Few towns in England can boast a greater antiquity or a more stirring history than Shrewsbury. The undulating irregularity of its streets and the graceful winding of the river combine to make the town especially attractive. The town's skyline is enhanced by the elegant spires of St Mary's and St Alkmund's, both built on the foundations of Saxon churches. The round structure in the centre of the photograph is the old water tower, which was situated between St Mary's Street and Butcher Row. It served the town well until the new one was opened at Shelton in 1935. In the top left-hand corner we can see part of the old cattle market in Raven Meadows.

Introduction

Very little is known of Shrewsbury's ancient history. There is no evidence of Roman settlement, their main centre of activity being focused on Viroconium 6 miles to the east. With the collapse of Rome came the invading hordes from across the sea and, although Viroconium remained inhabited for a number of years, it soon became obvious that a more secure site was needed.

The area which is now Shrewsbury offered numerous advantages. It is situated inside a horseshoe bend of the River Severn where the land rises steeply from a low and formally marshy riverside to a saddle of two small hills. The only land entrance, to the north, was very narrow and steep. It also had the benefit of two natural fords across the river on which the Welsh Bridge and English Bridge are now built. The name given to this early settlement was Pengwern, meaning the 'hill of the alders'.

Under the Saxons Shrewsbury enjoyed a great deal of prosperity. Five churches were founded, a flourishing market was established and a mint was set up. The first written evidence of the town comes in a document dated AD 901 when it was known as Scrobbesbyrig. The Scrobbes element refers to a hill covered in scrub, while the byrig implies some sort of fortification.

At the time of the Conquest the Earldom of Mercia belonged to Edwin who opposed the invasion, but after the defeat he submitted to William and was allowed to keep his lands. The following year a revolt took place in which Edwin played a leading part. He was killed and William transferred the earldom to Roger de Montgomery who became the first Norman Earl of Shrewsbury in 1074. One of Roger's first acts was to rebuild the castle in the motte and bailey style. He also founded Shrewsbury Abbey in 1083 with an endowment that brought in an annual rent of £12. In 1094 he entered the Abbey as a lay brother and died there three days later.

Under the Normans Shrewsbury developed into one of the principal towns of The Marches, as a fortress against Welsh incursions into England and a place from which the King could mount attacks into the Principality. Fighting with the Welsh intensified during the early part of the thirteenth century and as a result Henry III commanded that the town be enclosed with a wall of stone. During the reign of Edward I, Prince Llewellyn ap Gruffydd was slain at Builth and his brother David was captured and brought to Shrewsbury in chains. A Parliament was assembled at the Abbey in September 1283 where David was tried for treason and sentenced to death. The Parliament was significant for the fact that commoners were allowed to attend for the first time.

After the subjugation of the Welsh, Shrewsbury's military importance declined and the town developed into a commercial centre for Welsh wool. Trade flourished and in 1334 it was one of the richest provincial towns in the country. Trade fluctuated during the next two centuries but reached its peak around 1600. The Draper's Guild, who regulated the wool trade, were at the height of their prosperity at this time and some of their members were among the wealthiest citizens of Shrewsbury. Many of the timber-framed buildings we have today originate from then.

The tranquillity of the town was interrupted by the Battle of Shrewsbury in 1403.

Henry IV put down an insurrection lead by the Percy family of Northumberland. The battle raged for several hours with heavy losses on both sides including Henry Percy, known as Hotspur. Towards the end of the fifteenth century Shrewsbury once again became the focus of domestic affairs when the gates of the town were closed against the army of Henry Tudor who was claiming the throne from Richard III. However, Henry was allowed free passage after promising no harm would come to the town or its inhabitants.

Under the Tudors the Abbey was dissolved and the three lesser houses of the friars suppressed. However, during the reign of Edward VI the town was granted a charter to found a Royal Grammar School. At the outbreak of the Civil War in 1642 the town was loyal to the King but fell into the hands of the Parliamentarians in 1645.

With the Restoration Shrewsbury attracted less attention from London and began to settle into the role of regional capital and the centre of social and economic life. This role was developed during the eighteenth century with the town hosting a variety of social functions and supplying a large hinterland with goods and other services. A number of the county's leading families had homes in Shrewsbury and many of the elegant town houses in Belmont and Swan Hill were built at this time. The main social events revolved around the Lion Hotel with its Assembly Room and elegant Adam-style ballroom.

Towards the end of the eighteenth century Shrewsbury established itself into a leading coaching town lying on the direct route from Shrewsbury to Holyhead. It also seemed possible that it would develop into a major textile town. A woollen mill was erected in Carline Fields in 1790 and adapted for cotton spinning in 1803. A flaxmill was opened in Ditherington in 1796. Designed by Charles Bage, it was the world's first iron-framed building. Two other mills were opened in Castlefields and on Kingsland. Another business to flourish was Hazeldine's Ironworks in Longden Coleham. Hazeldine worked closely with Thomas Telford on a number of projects including the Menai Bridge.

The railway arrived in Shrewsbury in 1848 with the opening of the line to Chester. By the end of the century Shrewsbury had rail links with most of the major towns and cities in the country and a great deal of trade was brought into Shrewsbury by this means.

Improvements to the town were carried out throughout the nineteenth century. In 1850 a cattle market was erected in Raven Meadows and in 1869 a new Market Hall was opened, bringing together all the smaller markets scattered around the town.

As the nineteenth century closed the first motorized vehicles appeared in Shrewsbury bringing problems to the medieval streets which have still not been successfully solved.

Throughout the 1950s and early '60s it became fashionable to pull down old buildings and level ancient sites, replacing them with concrete, steel and glass. Sadly Shrewsbury lost some fine buildings during this period. In 1963 the Civic Society was formed and they have been instrumental over the years in making the public aware of any dangers in town planning.

During the last two decades greater emphasis has been put on conservation and in developing the town into a tourist attraction. A great deal of restoration has been carried out on many historic buildings, the major museums have been updated and a number of streets have been pedestrianized, making Shrewsbury an exciting town to visit and a pleasant place to live.

David Trumper, 1994

The Town Centre

The castle was built overlooking Shrewsbury's most vulnerable point, the only land route into the town. The first evidence of a stone building is from the reign of Henry II when the inner bailey and the first main hall were built. In the reign of Edward I the hall was enlarged and the distinctive rounded towers added. After years of neglect Thomas Telford restored the castle in 1787 as a dwelling for Sir William Pultney. The memorial to William Clement, a former surgeon, mayor and MP for the town, was erected in 1874. The photograph was taken before the forecourt to the station was excavated.

Shrewsbury station was erected in 1848 as a joint station used by four companies. It was designed by Thomas Penson, a native of Shropshire, and built by Thomas Brassey. By the end of the nineteenth century the trade being brought into the town by railway grew rapidly and extra accommodation was needed. The authorities were faced with either rebuilding or extending the station. They chose the latter, and between the years 1901 and 1902 the forecourt was excavated to a depth of 12 ft. The basement was opened up and faced with new stone to provide a main entrance and space for booking, parcel and other offices under the platforms.

Shrewsbury School was founded by Edward VI in 1552. The buildings to the left of the tower were erected between 1627 and 1630 and bear the arms of Charles I. The stone wall fronting the street contained many names carved into the stone by the scholars. It was removed when the school vacated these premises in 1882 and has been re-erected at the new school on Kingsland.

This unique photograph looking up Castle Street towards Pride Hill was taken in July 1914. The flags were in honour of King George V's visit to the Royal Show. The horse and cart belonged to Rupert Peplow, a confectioner from Frankwell.

Castle Street, *c.* 1912. In the centre is the church of St Nicholas, which was built in 1867. On the right is Thorne's Mansion where the celebrated Mrs Fitzherbert was reputed to have been born. On the left is Palin's Cake Shop, famous for making the Shrewsbury cake. The shop was later run by Thomas Plimmer who continued to supply the cake. A 1921 advert proclaiming the cakes ended: 'Save Plimmer who alone of men/Can make the Shrewsbury cake again/Although lies Palin dead and cold/Kind fate to Plimmer left the mould/Ever unchangeable to make/Salopi's Pride, the Shrewsbury cake.'

Castle Street, *c.* 1925. The buildings on the left disappeared during the 1960s, making way for the extension of Marks and Spencer's and the building of Woolworth's and Littlewood's stores. Note the 'Big Hat', a gentlemen's outfitters run by Frank Newton.

Pride Hill, *c.* 1885. The street is named after the Pride family, wealthy merchants who had a shop and mansion in the area from the thirteenth century onwards. The boy is standing outside Mitchell's the ironmongers, whose shop was known as 'The Big Kettle'.

Street cleaning on Pride Hill, *c.* 1910. Boot's the Chemist was erected in 1902 and has been extended twice. It was designed to blend in with the older timber-framed buildings of the town, but unfortunately the architect chose a style more appropriate to Ipswich than Shrewsbury!

Pride Hill and Butcher Row, *c.* 1870. The Shropshire and North Wales General Supply Store was run by Mr Richard Binnall in the middle of the last century. It was taken over by Phillips & Co., grocers who had opened several other stores in the town by the 1950s. To the left of the store is a rare glimpse of the Greyhound, a public house from 1856 until 1896.

Butcher Row, *c.* 1914. The area was built up in the thirteenth century and was known as the Flesh Stalls or Shambles. An 1828 directory lists sixteen butcher's shops on Pride Hill, fifteen in Butcher Row and nine in Fish Street! As there was no abattoir at this time the animals would have been slaughtered on site.

Pride Hill, *c.* 1920. The timber-framed building was Morris's Café while the taller brick building was Morris's grocery store. E. Randles was known in the last century as Paris House. In 1892 they were agents for the 'Duchess', 'Bon Ton', 'Ideal', 'Igods' and 'New Flexible Hips' corsets. The site was redeveloped into a luxury store by Morris's in 1927.

The first post office in Shrewsbury opened in 1840 in a small room on the ground floor of a building in Dogpole. As business increased it moved first to the Corn Market in The Square and then to the ground floor of the Talbot in Market Street. These premises were purpose built in 1877. The top floor was supposed to incorporate a new income tax office but this never happened.

The wooden High Cross was erected at the top of Pride Hill as part of the celebrations to mark the 500th anniversary of the Battle of Shrewsbury in 1903. It is supposed to mark the spot where the dead body of Hotspur was exhibited to the townspeople after the battle. In the background is the mock Tudor Crown Hotel which was opened in August 1901. The shop to the left of the hotel was run by Vincent Crump, a confectioner, who was also able to provide the famous Shrewsbury cake. When Princess Victoria visited the town in 1832 it was noted that she was 'graciously pleased' to accept a box of cake from the mayor.

Church Street, *c.* 1910. The timber-framed building is now part of the Prince Rupert Hotel. It was built by William Jones, a lawyer, in the early part of the seventeenth century. He was known locally as Jones the Rich. The mansion is associated with Prince Rupert of the Rhine, a nephew of Charles I, who is said to have made his headquarters there during a visit to the town in 1644.

St Alkmund's Place. The buildings in the centre were demolished in the 1950s to give wider access from Butcher Row into St Alkmund's Place. The opening in the middle was known as Burial Shut, leading from Butcher Row into the graveyard. The Bear Steps complex on the left was saved and restored by the Civic Society in 1968.

The name Dogpole is derived from 'ducken', to stoop, and 'pole', a summit, and refers to a low gate in the town wall, which crossed the top of the street. The Old House was built in the fifteenth century for the Rocke family. Mary Tudor is reputed to have stayed there in 1526. The first house on the right was known as the Penitentiary and was once the home for the fallen women of the town. For a short time after 1840 it became Shrewsbury's first post office. Between 1867 and 1881 it acted as Shropshire's eye and ear hospital.

Wyle Cop originates from the Welsh 'hwylfa', a road leading up a hillside, and 'coppa', a summit. The buildings towards the bottom of the hill were built around 1460 by Thomas Mytton, a bailiff of Shrewsbury and sheriff in 1485. The house at the top of the hill is where Henry Tudor is reputed to have stayed while en route to Bosworth.

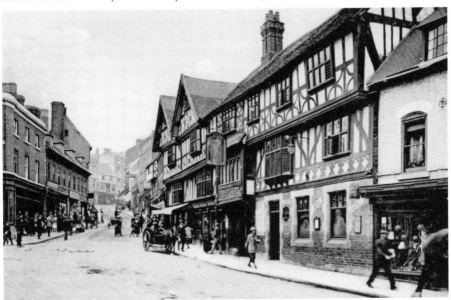

The Unicorn has been a hostelry since 1780. It was probably erected around 1603. Unfortunately the fine arch in the centre of the building has been removed to make it possible for high-sided vehicles to pass through.

This section of road known as Under the Wyle leads to the English Bridge. The mansion on the left was built by Thomas Sherar who was clerk to the Council of the Marches and an alderman of the town in the sixteenth century. It became one of the town's principal inns during the seventeenth and eighteenth century and was known as the Red Lion. The mansion ceased to be an inn around 1770 but part of it was converted into a public house in 1856 and named the Hero of Moultan. The name refers to Sir Henry Benjamin Edwards of Frodesley who gained fame for his courage and leadership in India. The building made way for Wales and Edwards garage. The site is now occupied by National Car Parks.

The Catholic Cathedral was designed by Edward Welby Pugin and was opened for worship on Wednesday 29 October 1856. The house on the far right was built by Jonathan Scott around 1701. It was purchased in 1821 to provide suitable accommodation for visiting judges.

Town Walls first appears as a street name in 1871. In 1851 this section of road was known as Tower Place. The watch tower dates from the thirteenth century and is the sole survivor of a number of towers that stood along the old town wall. Next to the tower is the Ebenezer Chapel, erected in 1834 by the Methodist New Connection.

The first Eye and Ear Dispensary was opened in 1818 in a private house on Castle Street. It moved to a house on Dogpole in 1867 and to this more permanent building in 1881. It is built out of Ruabon brick with terracotta dressing and was designed by C.O. Ellison of Liverpool. The £12,000 needed for its erection was raised by public subscription. The Countess of Bradford performed the opening ceremony, using a silver key.

Allatt's school, *c.* 1910. It was a charity school endowed by John Allatt in 1798 to cater for the education of forty girls and forty boys. Around 1900 the headmaster was J.W. Jepson. His daughter Kitty, standing on the extreme right of the photograph, was later a well-known dancer, running her own dance school in the town.

Princess Street was once known as Candlelanestrete, the site of the chandlers' shops. The round arch by the gas lamp leads into Peacock Passage, an ancient shut connecting Princess Street to High Street. It takes its name from an inn which stood at this end of the passage from 1780 until 1820. The YWCA was run by Miss B. Richards and was in existence from 1896 until 1910. The shop on the corner was run by J.T. Onions, who was also a boot repairer. It was later owned by Bert Dann, a well-known figure around the town in the 1950s and '60s.

Shrewsbury, Milk Street

Milk Street was once an extension of St Chad's Lane or Stury's Close, which followed the line of Belmont to Town Walls. The fine house on the left is Proude's Mansion, built in 1568 by George Proude, a local draper. Part of the mansion now houses the Old Post Office Hotel.

Fish Street, *c.* 1880. The street is first mentioned in the fourteenth century when boards, from which fish could be sold, were set up along the wall under St Alkmund's Church. The buildings on the left are known as the Bear Steps. They take their name from an inn that stood opposite on the corner of Grope Lane. The name of the inn can just be seen through the gas lamp. The people at the far end of the street are standing outside the cottage where John Wesley first preached to the people of Shrewsbury, in 1761.

High Street was once known as Gumblestolestrete, the site of the gumble or ducking stool. There was a pool at the side of The Square which was drained by an open stream that ran down to the Severn. It was in that pool that the scolds or people who cheated in the market were ducked.

This end of High Street was once occupied by cooks or bakers and known as Cook's, Baker's or Baxter's Row. Adams' shop was opened around 1905. In 1914 it was sole agent for the 'Ideal Cooker', which supplied great heat using very little coal.

The Square, *c.* 1890. The market moved here from St Alkmund's Square in 1261 and was built up and paved between 1272 and 1275. The cabbies' shelter in front of the Market Hall now stands by the main gate to the castle.

The inauguration of Lord Clive's statue took place on 18 January 1860, with this photograph probably being taken the same year. The statue, which stands around 9 ft high, was executed in bronze from a model by Baron Marochetti who copied the likeness from a painting by Nathaniel Dance. It was placed on a pedestal of polished Penrhyn granite. The total cost was 2,000 guineas, which was raised by public subscription.

During the 1940s and early '50s the bus station was in The Square. Even with the smaller amount of traffic on the road the area was very cramped and unsatisfactory. The Market Hall was built by the Corporation in 1596. Beneath the arches the corn market was held and the room above was used on Thursdays by the Company of Drapers to sell their Welsh wool and flannel clothes.

This was the second Shirehall to be built on this site. The first lasted only forty-nine years as the foundations were not deep enough. This building was designed in the Italian style by Sir Robert Smirke, and was completed in 1837 at a cost of £12,000.

The junction of The Square and Princess Street, c. 1890. The building with the tower is a rare view of the Working Men's Hall, opened in 1863. The foundation stone was laid by Mrs Wightman, a great temperance fighter and wife of the vicar of St Alkmund's. The building contained refreshment and reading rooms, baths and a lecture hall. During the 1950s the hall was used by Shrewsbury Repertory Company. It is now used as an antiques market.

Lloyd's Mansion was built by David Lloyd, a wealthy draper, around 1570. Around 1860 Joseph Della Porta extended his shop out of Princess Street and into these premises. This fine building was removed in the 1930s for the extension to the Shirehall and the timbers were left to rot in a builder's yard.

Robinson and Company have been trading in this elegant eighteenth-century Georgian town house for more than a century. A deed dated 1729 shows that the house was then occupied by Nathaniel Morris, a smith almost certainly working with silver. Between 1777 and 1787 the business was owned by Robert Richards, who later entered into partnership with Robert Morris. Morris traded for a while on his own, to be succeeded by Edward and James Robinson, who founded the firm we know today.

Mardol Head, *c.* 1910. Mardol Head was known as Lee Stalls, a name used right into the nineteenth century. During the eighteenth and nineteenth centuries a number of booksellers had shops in this area. The Royal Insurance Company built their new office on the corner of High Street between 1901 and 1902, on the site of their old fire station and the shop of O. Landon. Lloyds Bank moved into the building on the right around 1876, the same year as the frontage was extensively renovated.

The Theatre Royal was built in 1834 on the site of Charlton Hall. The ground floor contained several shops, an inn and the manager's house. The statues in the middle of the building represented Shakespeare and the comic and tragic muses. They were the work of a local sculptor, James Parry.

The interior of the theatre was highly ornamented. The ceiling had a dome in the centre with scrolls and medallions. From this were suspended magnificent gilt chandeliers. All the drapery was in gold and blue. The theatre later became a cinema, until it was gutted by fire in 1945.

Claremont Street, *c.* 1860. The buildings on the right were demolished in 1866 to make way for the new Market Hall. The house with the oriel window supported on posts is the King's Arms, built around 1615. It was once the residence of James Millington, the founder of Millington's Hospital in Frankwell. Before 1825 the street was known as Dog Lane.

The Market Hall site, *c.* 1866. The 1861 census shows there were over 300 people living in this area. There were also twenty-nine shops, sixteen brewhouses, eight warehouses, six workshops and two public houses, the King's Arms and the Mermaid. The businesses on the site included a tailor, a watchmaker, a hairdresser and a dentist.

The market was formally opened on 29 September 1869 by the mayor, Thomas Groves, and was followed by a large banquet held in the new corn exchange. The building was a mixture of architectural styles, and was built out of blue, red and white bricks with Grinshill stone dressing. It was replaced in the 1960s.

The Market Hall was described as spacious, with seventeen fruit, flower, confectionery and fish stalls set around the perimeter. The entire space in the centre of the hall was furnished with 114 benches and 57 double-sided seats to accommodate the users on market day. It was estimated in 1934 that on the main market days, Wednesday and Saturday, between 600 and 800 wives and daughters of farmers and market gardeners attended from a wide area to sell their produce.

Bridge Street was once known as Cripple Gate, a small opening in the town wall which led to a place by the river called the Mudholes, where an open sewer emptied into the Severn. The building on the right with the bell tower is St Chad's School.

Bridge Street to the Welsh Bridge, *c.* 1930. The buildings on the right were swept away in the 1930s to create an inner ring road and car parking spaces. The first timber-framed building is the Ship Inn. It was occupied by the Harwood family in the seventeenth century.

The junction of Bridge Street, Barker Street and St Austin's Friars, *c.* 1930. This area was also demolished for road widening. The shop on the left belonged to Sticky Turner, who sold excellent kindling. Two houses away is the Cosey Corner Fish and Chip Shop.

Hill's Lane was originally known as Knockin Street, which is derived from a medieval word meaning shaped like a bottle or cucumber. The Old Gullet Inn was the home of the Gullet Club, a notable institution founded in 1785. The club flourished in the last century, with MPs and prominent members of the public being among their number.

Mardol, *c.* 1914. In the last century Mardol was the collecting place for labourers who wished to be hired at busy times. The origin of the name is said to be an Anglo-Saxon word meaning 'devil's boundary'. The shop on the right was for many years Bromley's, the seed merchants. It was demolished in the 1960s to give wider access into Roushill. The timber-framed building on the left was restored in 1989.

Mardol, *c.* 1860. In 1860 this building was divided into two shops. The left-hand shop belonged to Martha Jones, a confectioner. Next door, Samuel Wilson was a provisions dealer. The ladies are standing at the entrance of Phoenix Passage. The name is taken from a Mr Phoenix who ran a bakery in the area. Before this it was known as Mason's or Shackleton's Shut. At the turn of the century it was known locally as The Crack.

Shrewsbury Cattle Market, *c.* 1930. Before 1850 cattle, sheep and pigs were sold in the main streets of the town. In 1847 Raven Meadows was chosen as the site for the new market. As it was very marshy ground the area was drained and raised several feet. The market was opened on 19 November 1850 at a cost of £20,000. It moved to Harlescott in 1959.

SECTION TWO

The Suburbs

Frankwell, *c.* 1940. This sixteenth-century building was once a public house known as The Bridge. It was first recorded in 1808 and delicensed in 1906. The building then housed a cycle shop run by F. Passant, who also made and sold the Salopia pram. By 1929 Foulkes, Gornall & Co. Ltd had opened their wireless shop there, and they in turn gave way to Medlicott Brothers, who continued to trade in the town until 1994.

Frankwell Quay was built in 1608 to cope with the growing trade brought into the town by barge. Several hostelries sprang up to cater for the needs of the bargemen. One was opened in this house as early as 1696 and was known as the White Horse. It continued to trade as an inn until the turn of the century, when it became the Model Lodging House, its owner guaranteeing well-aired beds. The passageway was called White Horse Passage. Before this it was known as Nettles Lane, after Roger Netelles, a glover who lived in the area around 1580.

Frankwell, c. 1890. The timber-framed building is known as the Fellmongers Hall, a place where sheep skins were brought from Wales for processing. The trade continued there until the 1960s. The large brick building, which was demolished to make way for a car park, was the home of the local sweep, Tommy Davies, for many years. The shop to the right of the Fellmongers was bought in 1869 by James Kent Morris, the founder of a local grocery empire which is still flourishing today.

Frankwell, *c.* 1900. Cattle being driven through the Little Boro' was a common sight on Tuesdays up until 1959, when the Cattle Market moved to Harlescott. On the right is the firm of Lewis & Frogett, the cycle specialists. Across the road they had an indoor cycling school where their latest models could be test ridden.

St George's School, *c.* 1890. A new elementary school was built on Millington's land at the rear of the infants' school and opened by John Bill on 28 June 1882. The children of the area were obviously a trial for the new master, who wrote in his log: 'The work sadly too much for the teaching power. So overworked that I can scarcely keep on.'

St George's Boys' School. The boys, with their headmaster Mr Bill, moved into a new school at the bottom of Copthorne on 30 August 1897. This photograph, taken in 1933, shows the boys of class I. Back row, left to right: R. Pugh, G. Morley, G. Chapman, W. Fallows, A. Ingram, W. McNamara, J. Lea, H. Morley. Second row: ? Watkins, W. Haddock, ? Deakin, G. Edwards, A. Williams, E. Piggott, ? Threadgold, R. Jones. Third row: W. Thomas, H. Corfield, E. Mullins, V. Buckley, S. Wem, K. Davies, H. Dilworth, E. Leake. Front row: -?-, E. Millington, G. Soden. St George's moved to a new site in Woodfield in the 1980s and the boys' school was demolished in 1994.

Copthorne Barracks, *c.* 1919. The building on this site was started in 1877, and the barracks were ready for occupation in 1880. On 30 December Depot Companies of the 43rd (Monmouthshire Light Infantry) and the 53rd (Shropshire Regiment) marched in from Shrewsbury station.

Port Hill, *c.* 1900. This road was known in the past as Boat House Bank, Bishop's Port Hill, Bishop's Castle or Pontesbury Road. In 1932, to stop confusion, the council decided that Port Hill started at the Boat House and finished at the junction of the new bypass. At this time Pengwern Road, which joins Port Hill with Copthorne, was just a lane – known locally as Love Lane.

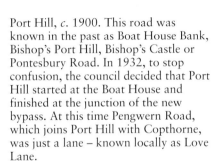

The Shoemaker's Arbour, Kingsland, *c.* 1870. The hall was octagonal and built of timber. The entrance was built of stone in 1679 at a cost of £28 6*s* 7*d*. The statues are of St Crispin and St Crispianus, the patron saints of shoemakers, and were added in 1684 along with the inscription 'We are but images of stone, do us no harm we can do none.' The gateway was moved to the Dingle in June 1880.

Meole Island, *c.* 1933. Shrewsbury bypass was opened on 23 May 1933 by the Princess Royal. The length of the road from Shelton to Emstrey is 4¼ miles. The Brooklands Hotel was opened in April 1931 to replace the Red Lion, which was demolished during the building of the new road.

The Limes, *c.* 1900. Samuel Pountney Smith, one of the county's most eminent architects, built himself this house in the second half of the last century. He incorporated materials collected from other buildings on which he had worked. Between 1951 and 1963 it was used as a boarding house for the Priory Girls' School.

Longden Coleham, *c.* 1930. People living in the area would have been used to seeing troops and military hardware moving around the Drill Hall. The men are part of the 240 Medium Battery, Royal Horse Artillery. The large gun is a howitzer.

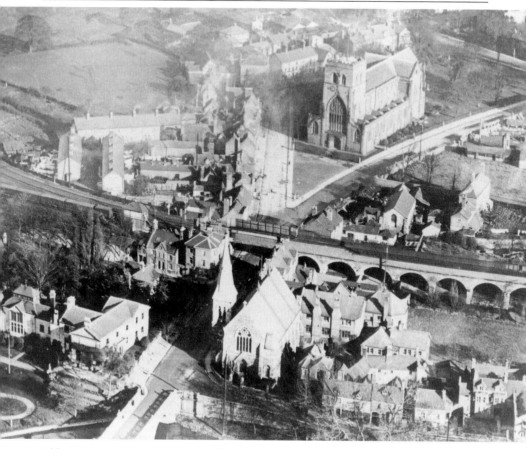

Abbey Foregate, *c.* 1918. Until 1835 the main road out of Shrewsbury passed to the left of the Abbey, but in that year Thomas Telford drove his new London to Holyhead road through the land to the south of the church, destroying what remained of the chapter house, cloisters and dormitory. The United Reformed Church at the bottom of the photograph was designed by G. Bidlake and opened in 1863. It too has been badly affected by the new gyratory road system, leaving it stranded in the middle of a large traffic island. This photograph was taken by one of the airmen training at the Observer School of Reconnaissance and Aerial Photography at Monkmoor Aerodrome.

The Abbey, *c.* 1880. This is a view to the north-east of the Abbey before restoration of the east end. The arches on either side of the east windows are now inside the main body of the church. The pointed arch leads into the new lady chapel while the rounded Norman arch leads into the vicar's vestry.

The Abbey station, *c.* 1870. The Potteries, Shrewsbury and North Wales Railway was opened in 1866. The line thrived in its early years but by 1880 profits had dropped, and it closed in 1882. The line was reopened in 1911 by the Shropshire and Montgomery Railway. During the Second World War it was used by the army to serve the Central Ammunition Depot at Nesscliffe.

Abbey Gardens, *c.* 1900. The lady is Miss Edith Wallett who ran a small school for young children at 167 Abbey Foregate. The large house was built by John Carline and became the town's Technical College in 1899. The site is now occupied by the Wakeman School.

Abbey House, *c.* 1890. This house was built for Thomas Jenkins, who was sheriff of the county in 1729, it remained in his family until 1861. Later it became part of the Abbey estates, and was due to become the residence of the Dean of Shrewsbury if the Shropshire Diocese had ever materialized.

Abbey Foregate, *c.* 1910. The column was built to commemorate the deeds of Shropshire's most notable soldier, Lord Rowland Hill. It cost £5973 13*s* 2*d*, which was raised by public subscription. While Lord Hill was fighting on the continent his Uncle Rowland, a preacher, was also making a name for himself in London. A poem written about them in a local paper ended: 'Surely old Rowland and Sir Rowland Hill/Have done enough to gain the world's good will/Each in his calling makes our foes retrench/One thumps the pulpit, while the other thumps the French.' The terrace of four houses set back from the road was built in the early part of the nineteenth century by one of the Carline family of stonemasons.

The Salop Steam Laundry was founded in the 1880s in an old mill which drew water from the Rea Brook. This photograph was taken in 1914 and shows the laundry's two modes of transport, both horse and motorized. In an advertisement for that year, customers were told that the laundry was situated in the open country and quite free from smoke and dust, and that all linen was dried in the open air whenever possible. The customer was also assured that no chemicals whatsoever were used. The general public could view the laundry at work on Wednesdays and Thursdays or at any other time by appointment. In 1914 the manageress was Miss M.A. McNaught.

The Armoury, *c.* 1916. In 1916 a group of local people cleaned and furnished the building to house Belgian families displaced by the war. In 1922 the building was bought by Morris's, taken down and re-erected near the Welsh Bridge to become their new bakery.

Whitehall was erected by Richard Prynce, a lawyer, between 1578 and 1582. A great deal of red sandstone from the dissolved Abbey is said to have been used, and according to local legend Prynce had the building white-washed to disguise the fact.

Monkmoor Road, *c.* 1906. The semi on the far left was the home of Wilfred Owen and his family from 1910. Wilfred was one of the greatest poets of the First World War and his death a few days before Armistice was a great tragedy. Before the war he enjoyed walks through the fields of Monkmoor to Haughmond Hill via Uffington Ferry.

Entrance to the Royal Show, 1914. The entrance housed the secretary's office, a post office and a ladies' room. It stood near the junction of Monkmoor Road and Crowmere Road. The houses in the background are on Crowmere Road.

The Model Farm, Monkmoor, *c.* 1914. One of the main attractions of the 1914 Royal Show was the Model Farm. Situated on the land near Abbots Place, the house was built of concrete from foundation to chimney-stack. Living accommodation consisted of a parlour, living room, scullery, larder and dairy on the ground floor, with three bedrooms and a box room on the first floor. The farm buildings were also constructed of concrete. There was a cowshed with standing for ten cows, a calf box, a mixing house, a stable, a pig house and a cart shed. After the show the farm was managed by a tenant for the County Council.

Castle Foregate, *c.* 1919. The Shrewsbury Industrial Co-operative Society opened their first shop at 70 Castle Foregate. By the First World War they had shops in Longden Road, Frankwell, Whitehall Street and Hotspur Street. The young man standing next to the manager on the step is Mr Harry Taylor who would, at a later date, take over as manager of this branch.

Cross Street, *c.* 1895. This view is taken from Chester Street. The cottages would have been demolished when the railway bridge was widened and a horse and carriage dock erected on the site. Note the gentlemen's urinal on the left.

Coton Hill, *c.* 1900. The timber-framed house is the birthplace of Admiral Benbow. Until 1900 a key hung on an old sycamore tree, said to have been put there by Benbow on the day he ran away to sea. It is now preserved in a box on the side of the house.

St Mary's Infant School, Coton Hill. For over forty years the mistress at the school was Miss L.J. Franklin. Around 1935 the school closed when Coton Mount School was opened and the children were transferred. At the same time Miss Franklin retired.

This unusual view was taken from Coton Hill railway bridge. On the horizon we see the prison, the castle, St Nicholas' Church, the library and, surprisingly, on the far right St Mary's spire. The area on the left was known as the Goods Deck. Trains were unloaded here into the Great Western yard; the goods were then distributed by road to local shops and businesses. The large chimney behind the signal belonged to the pumping station. The purpose of this was to maintain the level of water in the water columns used for filling the tanks on steam engines.

SECTION THREE
Inns and Breweries

The Lion is one of Shrewsbury's oldest hotels and is first mentioned in 1618. The Greek Doric columns to the doorcase and the model lion above are the work of Shrewsbury sculptor John Nelson, and were erected in 1777. Throughout the eighteenth and the early nineteenth centuries the hotel was the centre of social life for a wide area. The inn was closely associated with the coaching trade. By 1825 seven coaches ran daily to London and a further thirteen to various towns in the country.

The Raven, *c.* 1930. Accounts show that there was an inn on this site as early as 1587. The playwright George Farquhar is reputed to have written *The Recruiting Sergeant* while staying at the hotel in 1705. The building was demolished in 1959 to make way for Woolworth's and Littlewoods' stores.

The George, Shoplatch. This hotel served carriers to Knockin, Myddle, Westbury and Worthen. By 1851 it was the Shrewsbury terminus of the Prince of Wales coach to Aberystwyth and the Victoria coach to Hereford. The hotel was demolished in 1963.

The Market Tavern, *c.* 1870. These picturesque timber-framed buildings stood just below the Butter Market on Pride Hill. The tavern obviously takes its name from the market next door and was recorded as such from 1835 until 1861. The buildings were demolished and a purpose-built hotel called the Clarendon replaced them.

The Crown Hotel in St Mary's Street was first recorded in this Georgian house in 1780. Between 1832 and 1835 it was known as the Crown and Commercial and served county carriers throughout the nineteenth century. It was demolished in 1900 and a new hotel built in a 'mock Tudor' style was erected on the same site.

The building on the corner of Grope Lane and High Street dates from the end of the sixteenth century. A public house known as the Globe opened there around 1786. It had changed its name to the Cross Keys by 1820 and by the end of the last century it was known as Newman's Vaults. In 1891 a special feature of Mr Newman's stock was 'Vino de Pasto' supplied at 3s 4d a bottle or 40s per dozen.

The Slipper, in Barker Street, was first recorded as a public house in 1780. The name does not refer to a slipper worn on the foot but to the man who releases the greyhound from the leash in hare coursing. This building was demolished in 1939 after the new public house had been built at the rear.

The Bugle Inn was first recorded in Little or Paynes Lane in 1780. The narrow lane ran between Bridge Street and Hill's Lane and was later known as Bugle Lane, a name which is still commemorated in the Victorian Arcade. It was an alehouse which dealt mainly with outdoor trade. The premises were owned by the Drapers Company of London and their agent was Mr E.C. Peele of Cyngfeld, Kingsland.

The New Ship Inn was situated in a small yard to the side of Rowley's House and Mansion. It was called the New Ship to distinguish it from the Old Ship on Bridge Street. It became a public house in 1868 but was delicensed in January 1921. Mr Downes, the licensee, is the gentleman in the centre.

The Globe Inn. This public house was set up on Smithfield Road around 1861 and was first known as the Globe. It was run for many years by Eliza Cox, perhaps the lady standing at the door. It became the Smithfield in 1916 and was known under that name until 1959, when the market moved to Harlescott. It is now called the Proud Salopian, the inn sign portraying Alderman Thomas Southam, a brewer and former mayor of Shrewsbury.

The String of Horses, Frankwell. The house was built by John Worrell in 1576. It became a public house and was known as the Royal Oak, the Cross Keys and the String of Horses. It was delicensed in 1907 and used by the Co-op as a store until the 1960s.

Just five doors to the left of the last picture, in New Street, stood the Malt Shovel. The inn had only a short life (from 1874 until 1962), after which it was demolished to make way for a traffic island. The landlord between 1909 and 1917 was Samuel Hull, seen here with his wife and son. Up the passage next door to the inn was Hall's Dairy. The Hall family also ran the String of Horses.

The Bricklayer's Arms, Copthorne. The licensee was Mrs Sarah Pugh and the ladies on either side of the door are her daughters, Pat on the left and Sarah on the right. The little girl is Mrs Pugh's granddaughter Kitty. The public house was removed to its new site in the 1930s.

The Barge Inn stood to the right of the English Bridge. It was first recorded in 1870 and owes its name to its close proximity to the Severn and the craft used to carry goods on the river. The gate to the left leads to Marine Terrace.

The Dun Cow, Abbey Foregate. The animal over the door represents the murderous dun cow of Dunsmore Heath. According to legend a witch tried to milk the cow into a sieve, which so enraged it that it ran amok, until it was slain on Dunsmore Heath by the Earl of Warwick.

The Old House at Home, Castle Foregate. The inn was sandwiched between two other inns, the Thresher and the Eagle. It had only a short life, from 1871 to 1896. The lady on the left is Mrs Smith, a warden at Shrewsbury Prison.

The Woodman, Coton Hill, 1924. In 1900 the Woodman was listed as having eight rooms, four private and four public. It was an ale house and its customers were reported as being good. The licensee in 1924 was James Lewis, seen standing by the door with his wife.

The Quarry public house was demolished in the 1920s to widen the road from the Welsh Bridge to The Quarry. The large building at the rear is the Circus Brewery. The circus that gave its name to both an inn and the brewery was held in that building in the early part of the last century. The site is now occupied by Morris's.

The Old Salop Brewery, *c.* 1890. It was bought in 1845 by Thomas Trouncer. He became mayor in 1860 and was re-elected the following year. The cellars of the brewery opened on to the level of the courtyard so that casks could be rolled out without lifting. In an adjoining store were five enormous vats, each holding 5,000 gallons of beer.

Howard Street warehouse, *c.* 1900. The men standing outside are the staff employed by Southam's Brewery, which used part of the building as a bottling factory. The firm had offices on Wyle Cop and a main brewery in Chester Street.

Southam's Brewery, *c.* 1914. There was a brewery in Chester Street from the early part of the nineteenth century, run by Thomas Hawley. Thomas Southam started business in 1842 on Wyle Cop as a wine and ale merchant. Around 1852 he acquired these premises to brew his own beer. The business grew rapidly and within thirty years his company owned over twenty public houses in the Shrewsbury area. Apart from his business interests Southam served on the Borough Council for forty-four years; he also had the rare distinction of being elected mayor on four separate occasions. The site was redeveloped in 1983 into the Gateway Centre.

SECTION FOUR
Royal Events

The proclamation of George V was read in front of the Shirehall on Monday 9 May 1910. The High Sheriff Sir Raymond Wilson attended, supported by the Mayor and Corporation, the Borough Chaplain and the Under Sheriff, Colonel Cresswell Peele. Drawn up in front of the dais were a guard of honour provided by the KSLI, a cadet corps from Shrewsbury School and bands of the Shropshire Yeomanry and Borough of Shrewsbury. The proclamation was read by Colonel Peele.

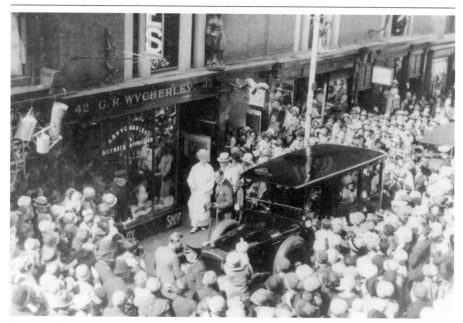

Queen Mary's visit, 1927. Wycherley's Old Curiosity Shop in High Street was a favourite place to browse. On this occasion the queen purchased some old English glass, a Sheraton cabinet and a choice Imari elephant. Great crowds followed her and traffic had to be re-routed.

The Prince of Wales visited Shrewsbury School on 21 June 1932 to celebrate the fiftieth anniversary of its removal to Kingsland. After laying the foundation stone of the old school wall he left on the ferry. Five 'eights' appeared on the river as a guard of honour.

King George V came to Shrewsbury on Friday 3 July 1914 to visit the Royal Show.
Before going to the showground he toured the town, met civic dignitaries and conferred
the title Royal on the Salop Infirmary. The guard of honour was provided by the KSLI
and mounted escort by the Shropshire Yeomanry.

On 20 April 1935 the Duke of York presented new colours to the 2nd Battalion KSLI in
The Quarry. The troops had left Whittington Barracks, Lichfield, on 16 April on a 200-
mile march that would take them through Staffordshire, Shropshire and Herefordshire.

The Princess Royal visited Shrewsbury in May 1933 to open the new bypass. She also visited schoolchildren in The Quarry for the Empire Day celebrations.

The paths of The Dingle were lined with girls each dressed in a delicately coloured frock and wearing a petal-shaped cap. Each child carried a basket of flowers, and as the princess passed gave a little curtsey. The princess was escorted by the mayor, Richard Mansell.

The Emir of Transjordan visited the town in 1934. He was described as 'a stately picturesque figure in his flowing eastern robes, with a silken headdress kept in place by a double wreath of camel hair and gold leaf'. After spending the night at the Raven the Emir visited a number of sites around the town, including the Castle, the RSI and The Quarry. He was escorted by Chief Constable Frank Davies.

The Sultan of Zanzibar made a brief visit to the town in 1929 while travelling from Stratford to Manchester. He was met by the chief constable and escorted to the Raven for lunch. At two o' clock he was taken to the castle to meet the mayor, Alderman Perks.

Queen Elizabeth visited the town on 24 October 1952. She came as part of the celebrations of Shrewsbury School's 400th anniversary and to open the new terrace on Kingsland. Arriving in Shrewsbury by train, she travelled around the area by car. She returned to the town centre via Frankwell and this view shows her car turning the corner at the bottom of New Street. All the people of the Little Boro' turned out to greet her and the main streets were full of flags and bunting. Notice the queen's entourage following down New Street in the reflection in the shop window.

SECTION FIVE

The Motor Car

Castle Foregate, *c.* 1920. By this date horse-drawn transport was dying out and the people of Shrewsbury were becoming used to the advent of the motor car. These taxi drivers wait patiently for customers on the station forecourt. The driver second from the left is Albert Preece, who drove for Painters for many years.

Mountford's Coach and Carriage Works on Dogpole was established in 1819. The building was converted into one of Shrewsbury's first garages, having connections with the Raven Hotel, which was beginning to cater for new trade brought in by the motor car.

Wither's Garage, Mardol Quay. Built in the middle of the last century, it was used for the manufacture of horse-drawn vehicles for both personal and commercial use. The building was quickly adapted for the motor car and continued to function until it was demolished in the 1930s.

Central Garage, Butcher Row. This site is now occupied by the public toilets. Shuker's traded there from 1896 until after the First World War. In 1914 they were agents for Belsize, Humber, Overland and Singer cars.

Greenhous' Garage, Greyfriars, 1929. During the 1920s this firm staged a number of motor shows. Exhibits included Rolls Royce, Bentley, La Selle and Buick cars. For the 1929 show a Chevrolet six cylinder truck, fully laden, became the first motorized vehicle to ascend the Wrekin.

This accident on Wyle Cop occurred on Monday morning 16 September 1940 and involved five vehicles. A lorry driven by a Liverpool man collided with a stationary car owned by William Nicholas of Belle Vue. Mr Nicholas was able to jump out but his car was pushed into another, which in turn collided with a railway lorry driven by a Mr Watkiss of Bishop Street. A bicycle owned by Harry Craven of Rea Street was also involved. Thankfully none of the drivers was injured. In the early days of motoring it was not unusual to see cars rolling driverless down the Cop, their handbrakes having failed on the steep incline!

SECTION SIX
The River Severn

The Welsh Bridge was built in September 1795 downstream of the old structure. It was designed by Tilley and Carline and cost £8,000. Under the first arch you can see the fence to the town tip, set up in 1824 and known to the locals as the Muck Yard. Beyond that was Penny Hedge where the women of Frankwell would do your washing and hang it on the hedge to dry, for just 1*d*.

The Boathouse Hotel has been an inn for over 200 years. It was once a pest house, a place where people who contracted the plague could be isolated. A manually operated ferry ran from this site until 1922, when the Port Hill Bridge was opened.

The Riverside Café at Shelton was owned by William Abley, the licensee of the Boathouse Hotel. From the Boathouse you could hire a rowing boat to row up to Shelton where you could purchase a wide variety of refreshments. Motor launches like the *Lady Sue*, in the last photograph, were also available for the same trip.

Pengwern Boat Club was founded in February 1871. The club took its name from an earlier organization, formed in 1835 and reputed to be the first rowing club in the country. It moved to these premises in 1881.

Dress regulations were very strict in the early years. Racing competitors had to wear a white vest which completely covered the chest. Loose trousers could be worn or knickerbockers which covered the knee. As well as racing boats the club maintained a number of pleasure boats, which enabled members to take their families for trips upstream in the summer.

Cooper's Boats, *c.* 1900. This business was established by Richard Ellis in 1859 and flourished for around a hundred years. It was taken over by Mr George Cooper in 1906. In the 1920s a fleet of punts, pleasure, racing and fishing boats could be hired from under the Kingsland Bridge. Mr Cooper also ran a workshop and showroom in Coleham, and employed a large workforce to undertake the building and repairing of boats – either on the premises or on site.

The Kingsland Bridge, *c.* 1890. The bridge is an iron structure resting on stone piers with a single span of 212 ft. It was completed in 1881, but not opened to traffic until 28 July 1882, which coincided with the official opening of the new Shrewsbury School.

The Cann Office Ferry was opened around 1750 and formed a direct route from Kingsland to the town centre. In the last century it was known as Burr's Boat due to the close proximity of Burr's Leadworks. The ferry closed in 1893.

Severnside, *c.* 1910. Horses graze on a field now occupied by tennis courts. Along the line of the river are the young trees planted to commemorate Queen Victoria's Diamond Jubilee in 1897. Across the river are some buildings which stood near Burr's Leadworks.

The Franciscan Friars occupied this site from around 1245. Hawis, wife of Charlton, Lord of Powis, was a great benefactress and probably the founder of the friary. The Jesse window now in the east end of St Mary's is supposed to have decorated the church of the friary. The fragment of building still standing is thought to be part of the refectory.

The English Bridge, *c.* 1910. The bridge was designed by John Gwynn and opened to traffic in 1774. The scene was not always as tranquil. On one occasion a gentleman was fined 2*s* 6*d* for ferociously driving his horse and cart down Wyle Cop and over the bridge.

By the 1920s it was obvious that the bridge was unable to cope with the growing amount of motorized traffic wanting to enter the town by that route. A plan was devised to rebuild the bridge, and work commenced in 1925. For two years all traffic was diverted over the temporary wooden bridge.

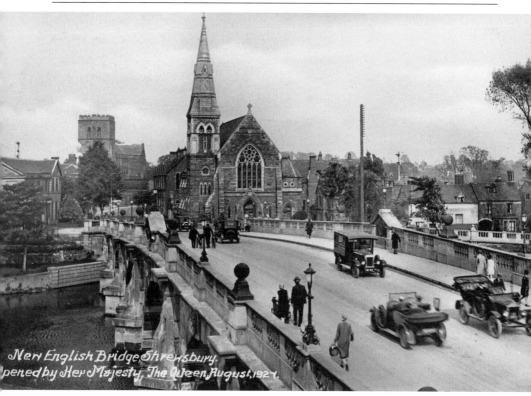

New English Bridge, Shrewsbury.
opened by Her Majesty, The Queen, August 1927.

The reconstructed bridge was due to be opened by the Prince of Wales on 27 October 1927, but because of the sudden death of his uncle, the Marquis of Cambridge, this was postponed. The Borough Council then wrote to Queen Mary to ask if they could use a plaque stating that she was the first person to cross the new bridge in a car on 13 August. She agreed, and a circular panel was inserted over the centre arch.

The watergate at the foot of St Mary's Water Lane is the sole surviving thirteenth-century gate of the town's defences. It is through this gateway that the Parliamentarians gained entry to the town in 1645. The Dominican Friary stood to the right of the gate. After the Dissolution, their land was laid out as a bowling green for the members of the Council of the Marches.

The Severn Viaduct was completed before the opening of the Shrewsbury to Birmingham railway in June 1849. Between 1899 and 1902 two iron girder bridges were built on either side of the original viaduct to provide space for extra lines and to extend the platforms out over the river. Note the Severn Junction signal box straddling the old bridge.

The Weir, Shrewsbury

The weir was constructed in Castlefields between 1910 and 1912 to maintain a minimum height of water around the town. The weir is 195 ft in length and was attached to the river-bed by green heart wood. Work was severely hampered in December 1910 by a flood which reached a height of 16 ft above normal. In the background is the Castle Walk suspension bridge opened in November 1910 by the mayor, Councillor Blower. It connected Cherry Orchard with Castlefields and replaced a ferry that ran from the bottom of Bradford Street.

SECTION SEVEN
Floods

The flood of January 1899 has been particularly well recorded and the next eight photographs show the effect it had on the town. The north side of the Abbey is always one of the first areas to suffer and several inches of water entered the church itself. The man on the left is the Revd Mr MacNab, curate of the Abbey, who used to row around the Foregate offering assistance to his parishioners.

The lofty arches of the English Bridge were high enough to cope with this flood when the river at its peak reached a height of 17 ft 6 in.

Wagons and cabs easily negotiated the flood waters at Coleham Head. Benches and planks were erected for pedestrians and pews were requisitioned from the Congregational Church.

People using cabs in Coleham were forced to hold their feet up on the seats opposite. One young man had the cheek to try and ride through the flood on a bike, but came to grief opposite the Swan and found himself up to his waist in water.

Like a huge lake, the water covers a great deal of Coney Green in the foreground and the whole of Severnside below Town Walls. In the top left above the flood plain are The Crescent and the Catholic Cathedral.

The waters of the flood completely surrounded the old lime trees in The Quarry and reached right up the steps of the Pengwern Boat Club. The steward of the club at this time was Mr Hoare, an ex-champion sculler.

The only planks laid in Chester Street were as far as the Rifleman Inn and were probably put down by the landlord for the benefit of his customers. During these floods the Corporation was praised for the way it dealt with the flood emergency.

Frankwell always suffers badly in floods and 1899 was no exception. On the Monday of the flood, a young Frankwell bride found the ground floor of her house was completely submerged. The determined girl left for the church through the bedroom window and was rowed to dry land. After the ceremony she returned by the same route with her new husband and guests for the wedding breakfast. The beautiful cast-iron urinal disappeared during the First World War. It was known locally as the Frankwell Relief Centre.

Coton Hill to the County ground, Frankwell, *c.* 1941. In the background are the Barge Cottages. They stood to the left of the barge gutter, cut to take river craft, when the main channel of the river was blocked by a fish weir.

Mardol Quay, *c.* 1946. The floods of 1946 saw the river rise to a height of just over 19 ft at the Welsh Bridge. Gethin's Garage was set up in 1920 and was in operation for around forty years. The Hill's Arms was demolished around 1952 to allow wider access to Smithfield Road.

Mardol, *c.* 1941. During these floods the river rose to 18 ft above normal. Quite large areas at the bottom of Mardol were submerged, including the King's Head. Outside the Empire Cinema a sign stated that non-swimmers were not allowed in the first six rows!

Phoenix Passage, *c.* 1936. This area of the town is always one of the first to suffer, the water rising up through the drains. The *Chronicle* described this scene as reminiscent of a mini Venice.

Frankwell, *c.* 1936. This was the first major flood to affect the town since 1929. The water rose quickly after a rapid thaw of snow followed by heavy rain. At the Welsh Bridge a 9-in rise was recorded in just one hour. Standing in the doorway is Mrs Taylor and her daughter Mrs Edwards. To the left of the door is another of Mrs Taylor's daughters Mrs Braddick and in front of her is Vera Evans. In the bedroom window is Mrs Thomas, and Bert Rhodes is standing on the extreme left.

SECTION EIGHT

The Quarry

Central Avenue, *c*. 1900. The Quarry was once known as Behind the Walls. Its modern name comes from the stone quarrying carried out in The Dingle and around the area by the swimming baths. The lime trees along the side of the river are said to have been planted by a local nurseryman, Thomas Wright, in 1719. The other walks were treated the same way a few years later.

The Dingle is the centrepiece of The Quarry. This view of the new rock garden was taken in 1924. The garden was built by Elliott's of Stevenage and was a gift of the Horticultural Society. It cost £693 12s 2d.

The lead statue of Hercules is said to have been cast in Rome over 350 years ago. It stood outside Condover Hall until 1804. After some years in a builder's yard it was bought by W.H. Griffith, the governor of the prison, and erected on Howard's Bank. Around 1851 it was presented to the town and removed to the entrance of The Quarry. When the new gates were erected in 1881 the statue was removed to its present site.

The Jubilee Baths, *c.* 1910. The foundation stone was laid on Whit Monday 1893, following a suggestion in 1887 that baths should be built to commemorate Queen Victoria's Golden Jubilee. The structure contained two swimming pools and several slipper baths. It was built of red brick and Grinshill stone dressing. The mayor and 250 guests attended a special opening lunch in 1894. Other events to mark the occasion were a fête, sports day and an angling competition.

The Flower Show was set up as an alternative to the old Shrewsbury Show which, by the middle of the nineteenth century, had fallen into disrepute. As well as flowers and music the two day show has introduced many new attractions over the years to entertain the whole family.

On 17 August 1927 Queen Mary graced the show with her presence. She was escorted around The Quarry by the chairman, Mr William Adams, and the president, Colonel Heywood-Lonsdale. Her delight was obvious and she was heard to remark on several occasions: 'What a wonderful sight'.

This area between The Quarry Lodge and the river has always been used for entertainment. The stage show brought together some of the best music hall acts from around the world.

This was the view from the stage, *c.* 1912. A packed audience is eagerly anticipating the next act, a fresh performance being guaranteed every fifteen minutes.

High-wire acts were introduced to the show in 1880. Gasps of admiration could be heard across The Quarry at the breathtaking feats of the performers as they displayed their skills to a captive audience. Artists who took part in those early shows included The Brothers Wichmann, Lolo, Sylvester and Lola, and The Great Caicedo, King of the Wire.

The first balloonist was James Whelan from Huddersfield who attended the show in 1880. At his thirteenth show in 1893 he broke his pelvis when landing. He was taken to the Salop Infirmary where he died on 2 September, aged just fifty-three.

Churches and Chapels

St George's Choir, *c.* 1934: Back row, left to right: H. Hall, E. Rowson, A. Wilcox, F. Davies, D. Groves, E. Lambert, G. Dawes, W. Trapp, E. Forrester, R. Lee. Seated: W. Culliford, ? Gough, A. Williams, S. Ralphs (choirmaster), Revd Mr Agnew, D. Wright, R. Williams, H. Brooks, W. Modlen. Front row: G. Thomas, W. Gale, E. Hall, F. Bowers, E. Williams. At the time of their retirement from the choir Messrs Rowson, Groves and Davies had recorded over 179 years service between them.

St Mary's is the most beautiful of all the town's churches. Founded in the tenth century, it has been altered on numerous occasions and a number of styles can be seen within its fabric. The tower, which is one of the tallest in the country, reaches a height of 222 ft. The greatest treasure the church possesses is its fine collection of stained glass dating from the fourteenth century, including examples from Belgium, Holland and Germany.

This procession entering St Mary's Church is a Lichfield Diocesan Missionary Festival in the early 1920s. The figure behind the boy scout is Bishop Lionel Crawford. Behind him wearing cape and mitre is Bishop Kempthorne, Bishop of Lichfield.

Old St Chad's, *c.* 1900. At the turn of the century the crypt of the old church was excavated and stonework revealed that a building of Saxon origin had stood on this site. The crypt was known as the 'Dimery', a dark place for storage.

The Church of St Julian dates from the tenth century. It was rebuilt, with the exception of the tower, in the classical style in 1750. The church was made redundant and is now a craft centre. All that remains of the old church of St Alkmund is the tower and spire. The main body of the church was removed in 1792 after the fall of St Chad's, the church council fearing for its safety. They need not have worried as gunpowder had to be employed to loosen parts of the structure.

A garden fête in aid of the Abbey organ fund was held in July 1920 in the Abbey Gardens. The young lady presenting the bouquet to Mrs R.E. Jones, the mayoress, is Edith Woodnorth. The Woodnorths had close connections with the Abbey, several of the family serving as churchwardens. They also ran a grocer's shop in the Foregate as well as the Bull Inn.

The Church of the Holy Spirit was erected in 1936 in the rapidly expanding suburb of Harlescott. It cost £2,500 with a further £30 for fixtures and fittings. A new church was opened on another site in the 1960s and this building was transformed into a social club.

The first Unitarian Church was built in High Street in 1691. During the Jacobite riots of 1715 a mob gathered outside the church and started pulling it down. The present building was erected in 1839 but was extensively altered in 1885 and 1903.

The first Methodist Chapel was set up in the Shearmen's Hall, Milk Street, in 1761, the rent for the building being paid for by John Appleton. Twenty years later he built this chapel in Hill's Lane at his own cost. It was opened on 27 March 1781 by John Wesley. The building was demolished in 1937.

The Baptist Church, Claremont Street, *c.* 1870. This church was opened in 1780 and enlarged in 1810. It is thought that the building was once used as an arsenal before its conversion. A new church was erected on this site in 1878.

The foundation stone of the new Coton Hill Congregational Church was laid in July 1908. The building it replaced was the Royal Baths, opened in 1831. In 1851 the baths offered hot air, vapour, shower, warm, salt, medicated and fresh water baths, as well as a pleasure bath large enough to allow people to learn to swim.

People at Work

The Racecourse, Monkmoor, 1914. The Royal Show was held in Shrewsbury between 30 June and 4 July. For several weeks a large workforce had been preparing the ground for what was to prove a very successful event. Record prize money of £11,700 attracted an unusually high number of 3,394 entries of livestock. The town had hosted the show on two previous occasions, 1845 and 1884, and was to do so again at Sundorne in 1949.

Chef Hug was born in the Ukraine and worked for many years as head chef at Morris's Restaurant. The cake in the shape of Morris's main shop on Pride Hill is probably for the window display that he always created for Flower Show week. The building is a copy of Blickling Hall in Norfolk.

Livesey's Composing Room, *c.* 1910. This printing firm was founded by a Mr Wardle on Pride Hill in 1843. The business was transferred to Cross Hill around 1880 and was taken over ten years later by Joseph Livesey, a native of Preston.

The final phase in the rebuilding of the English Bridge was carried out by the Birmingham & Midland Counties Val de Travers Paving Co. They laid the top road surface with natural rock asphalt from Switzerland.

Benyon Street, Castlefields, *c.* 1900. Harry Holl stands proudly outside his family business. In the doorway is his wife, holding their daughter May. Sitting in the cart beside an apprentice is their son Harry. The shop was later run by George Lewis until it closed in the 1930s.

Shrewsbury's worst ever rail crash occurred on the night of 15 October 1907 when the Crewe to Swansea mail train was derailed just outside the station. The engine left the rails on the steep curve by Crewe Junction signal box, its wheels ploughing a deep furrow before falling over and taking most of the coaches with it. The final death toll was eighteen with another forty seriously injured.

Shrewsbury's first infirmary was housed in a mansion belonging to the Kynaston family. It was opened on 25 April 1747 and was reported to be only the fifth in operation at that time. This building was erected on the same site and opened in September 1830 at a cost of £16,000.

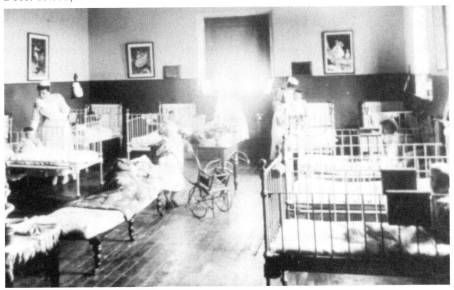

It took three years to build, the patients being housed during this time at the House of Industry on Kingsland. The hospital closed in November 1977 and the building has been transformed into a shopping centre and luxury apartments.

The Fire Brigade of the Alliance, Salop and Shropshire & North Wales Fire Office, *c.* 1900. Before 1917 there were two fire fighting services in Shrewsbury. They were both provided by insurance companies and were completely independent of each other. The site of this station was Franklin's Livery Stables on Cross Hill. These men and their horse-drawn steam engine were under the command of Edward Vaughan, an active man, who remained in the service until he was seventy-five years old.

The inscription on this photograph was 'The New Fire Escape for Shrewsbury Around 1870'. The ladder was kept under the Market Hall in The Square and could be moved quickly around the town in an emergency. The men of the Alliance Brigade are practising their rescue technique on the steep slope of Wyle Cop.

Cross Hill, *c.* 1960. The escape ladder has changed hardly at all and the firemen still practise their rescue. Live rescues are now banned and the 'victim' has been replaced with an 11-stone dummy. The drill is taking place outside the fire station and is supervised by Dennis Trumper. Nick Morris holds the levers of the 50-ft ladder, while Jim Jones perfects the rescue with a fireman's lift.

This photograph taken on Cross Hill in 1930 shows a landmark in the history of the Borough Police Force, the first car to go on active service. The two police officers are PC Othen (left), who was the driver, and PC Len Dyke. Another great innovation of 1930 was the erection of four street police boxes on Monkmoor Road, The Mount, The Column and in St Michael's Street.

People, Personalities and Parades

Mrs Marion Wallace Cock became the first lady mayor of Shrewsbury in 1934. She was born in Chile and came to Shrewsbury after her marriage to James Cock, head of a large tannery. She was always very keen on local affairs. After the premature death of her husband, she managed to continue the interest as well as raise six children and run the family business. She is with the Borough Police and Chief Constable Frank Davies.

On St David's Day 1937 the Welsh flag was hoisted over Shrewsbury Castle for the first time since 1485. Madame Dobson in national costume sang, accompanied by Elsie Thomas on harp. The mayor is Charles Beddard and to his left is Clement Davies MP, who hoisted the flag.

The topping-out ceremony of Shelton Water Tower was carried out in August 1934 by the mayor, Richard Mansell, and Alderman Beddard, chairman of the Watch Committee. The 80-ft tower holds 500,000 gallons of water. The completed works were opened the following year by Viscountess Bridgeman.

Marching to war, August 1914. The 1st/4th battalion KSLI were mobilized at the Drill Hall, Coleham on 5 August and were dispatched immediately to Barry Docks, under the command of Colonel J.H. Howard-MacLean. They were marched to the station, headed by their band.

The Shropshire Home Guard celebrated their third anniversary in May 1943 with a march through the county town. The salute was taken by the mayor, Captain Harry Steward. Marching down High Street are the 1st Battalion (Shrewsbury) and the 9th Battalion (GPO) of the Shropshire Home Guard.

Frankwell ARP Wardens, *c.* 1943. The wardens were responsible for Frankwell and parts of Copthorne. They met on two nights a week for training as well as reporting for two duties. Occasionally social evenings were held in the Cross Guns, New Street. From the left: F. Jones, B. Thomas, Mr Hughes, Mr Knight, Mr Major, C. Jones, F. Croxton, L. Cuniffe, Mr McNamara, C. Whitehead, T. Peters, Mr Hicks, B. Chant, E. Reece, Mr Gibbs, F. Lakelin, F. Jones. Mr McNamara was Mayor of Shrewsbury in 1953.

Shrewsbury Golf Club, c. 1930. Golf was once played at Hencote but by the turn of the century a new course had been opened at Meole Brace. An army hut was purchased as a club house in 1919 and provided ladies' and gents' changing rooms, a tea room and catered for the club's social events.

Wyle Cop Gym Club, c. 1930. The club were famous for their acrobatic and gymnastic displays performed at events around the county. Sam Powell, seated in the middle row second from the left, was their trainer. On the right of the back row is George Dawes, and in the centre of the front row is Ted Evans.

SHREWSBURY TOWN F.C. (Season 1911-12)

W. Adams   P. Higley   W. Jones,   W. Scarratt, P. Norris, C. Morgan, A. Hemmings, R. E. Rumsey,
(Trainer)   (Chairman)   (Captain)

F. W. Jones,   H. Slater,   J. Gorman,   F. Foxall,   R. Ince (Treasur

J. Bridge,   E. Tremlett,   A. Davies,   W. H. Peplow

Shrewsbury Town Football Club was founded on 20 May 1886. They played their home matches on the Racecourse until 1889 when they moved to another site in Monkmoor known as Ambler's Field. In 1893 they moved to Sutton Lane and two years later to a field near the Barracks in Copthorne. In 1910 the club transferred to their present site at the Gay Meadow. They played their first match there on 3 September against Wolves Reserves and lost 2–1.

The Rt Revd Samuel Webster Allen was Shrewsbury's fourth Catholic bishop between 1897 and 1908. During his time as bishop twelve new churches and ten new missions were opened in the diocese. A requiem mass was held for Bishop Allen at the Cathedral on Town Walls.

The funeral cortège of the Marquis of Cambridge, October 1927. The marquis died at the Salop Nursing Home, Quarry Place, after a short illness. The funeral was at Windsor and he was escorted out of the town by the Borough Police Force. A guard of honour of Shropshire Yeomanry lined the English Bridge.

Towards the end of the First World War, the people of Shrewsbury were privileged to witness several flying displays by intrepid airmen who manoeuvred their powerful biplanes to perform thrilling feats over the town. I believe this is Captain Collett, an old Salopian, who landed his plane on the school's cricket pitch in July 1918. Hundreds of people lined the banks of the Severn in the hope of an aerial display. They were not disappointed, as Captain Collett electrified the spectators by flying not once but nine or ten times under the Kingsland Bridge.

Shrewsbury Carnival, Pride Hill, 1933. The hospital carnivals were started in 1931 and in the first two years raised over £2,000 for local hospitals. The 1933 carnival attracted over 2,000 competitors. Two parades took place, one in the afternoon and a lantern procession in the evening. The Royal Welch Fusiliers are leading the parade.

Shrewsbury Carnival, Mardol Head, 1933. Miss Shropshire was Miss Kathleen Worsley of Much Wenlock. She and her forty attendants were driven through the town on two floats decorated in blue and yellow.

BORO' OF FRANKWELL.

The Little Boro' 2708

CARNIVAL ASSIZES

WILL BE HELD ON

FRANKWELL QUAY,

On CARNIVAL DAY, Sept 15th, 1938.

at 1-30 p.m.

NOTORIOUS PRISONERS FOR TRIAL.

TICKET OF ADMISSION - - 1d.

WE MUST SEE YOU AT THE ASSIZES.

Proceeds to Hospital Carnival Fund.

Frankwell always maintained its right to hold its own carnival. A large banner was placed over the Welsh Bridge with the motto 'Out of the Vale of Sin (Shrewsbury) Into the Land of Purity (Frankwell)'. Anyone who lived outside the Little Boro' had to pay 1*d* for the privilege of entering.

Frankwell Jazz Band, Chester Street. The band was founded in 1933 by Len and Emily Davies. They were very successful, winning the title of Midlands County Champions in 1937. To pay for their instruments and uniforms they held spotted dick and cocoa evenings in St George's Parish Hall.

Frankwell Carnival, 1935. This float depicts the opening of the Frankwell Water Works. Frankwell's first 'lady' mayor J. Jennings, with the help of the mayoress Natty Price, performed the ceremony. After turning the key a stream of dark brown fluid with a good head on it emerged from the tower. After taking samples both the mayor and corporation seemed satisfied with the liquid. Principal characters include: W. Steventon (chairman), N. White (water engineer), E. Welsby (borough engineer), C. Morley (chief engineer). Also on the float are G. Bebbington, W. Tisdale, T. Worrell, F. Braddock, S. Askew, T. Howells, H. Burgin, G. Evans, J. Braddick, J. Jones and J. Peplow.

Acknowledgements

The photographs in this book are taken from slides and photographs which I have collected over the past twenty years. This collection would not have been possible if it were not for the kindness of so many people who have located and supplied me with material. I would like to thank everyone listed below very much for their generosity. There are probably others whose names I have not included as my hobby only started on a small scale and I did not realize that it would grow to the size it has reached today. It is for this reason that I did not keep early records as I thought I would be able to remember anything that was loaned or given to me. Nevertheless I am greatly indebted to all those who have helped me over the years.

Abbeycolor • Mr A. Bertenshaw • Miss Breeze • Mr D. Carter • Mrs Caswell
Mr H. Corfield • Mr L. Davies • Mr & Mrs I. Davies • Mr & Mrs Evans
Mrs G. Fallows • Mrs C. Hole • Mrs L. Horler • Mrs F. Jones • Livesey Ltd
Local Studies Library • Mr J. Mabbot • Mrs M. Moran • Morris & Co
Mrs J. Mumford • Mr G.A. Parfitt • Mr R. Pilsbury • Mr J. Powell • Mrs Preece
Miss M. Rollings • Mrs M. Thomas • Mr S. Turner • Mr D. Walley
Mrs J. Watson • Mr W. Woodnorth • Mr C. Worth

I would like to express my thanks to Tony Carr and his staff at the Local Studies Library. They have assisted me greatly over the years and have always been friendly, helpful and patient when dealing with my enquiries. A special thanks to Madge Moran for the help and advice she gave me at the beginning of this project and to Mr Geoff Parfitt for all his help and encouragement. There are many more people who have shared their memories and experiences with me since I first took an interest in local history, and this information too has proved to be invaluable – thank you. I am also grateful to Mr Robert Evans of Abbeycolor for his help in preparing the photographs for this publication.